AF255892

SEASPRAY 17

OCEAN PHOTOGRAPHY & HAIKU POETRY

KIAN BATES & DANNIKA PATTERSON

For my ocean-loving little brother, Adam Maxwell Haling. DP
For my children, Kayla and Cody Bates, two fine examples of the next
generation of custodians of our ocean: enjoy it, respect it, protect it. KB

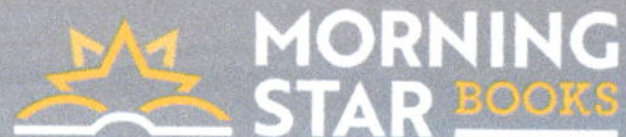

First published by Morningstar Books
51 Steel Street, Capalaba, Qld 4158 Australia

This publication is copyright. Apart from any use as permitted under the Copyright Act 1968, no part may
be reproduced by any process without prior written permission from the publisher.

Requests and enquiries concerning reproduction should be addressed to Morningstar Books.

Photography © Kian Bates, Raw Edge Photography, 2019
Text © Dannika Patterson, 2019
Raw Edge Photography website: www.rawedgephotography.com.au
Dannika Patterson website: www.dannikapatterson.com
Underwater model: Emira Harris

Morningstar Books Website: www.morningstarbooks.com.au

First published 2019

National Library of Australia Cataloguing-in-Publication entry:
Creator: Patterson, Dannika, author
Other Creator/Contributor: Bates, Kian, photographer
Title: SeaSpray17 / Dannika Patterson ; photography by Kian Bates

ISBN: 978-0-6485778-0-5

Target audience: Families, children ages 6 and up
Subjects: Poetry, Haiku, Photography, Ocean Photography, Australian Beaches

CONTENTS

Rise

At the ocean's edge

sun sets, wind drops, swell settles

and Foam Dancers rise.

Blueys Frothers

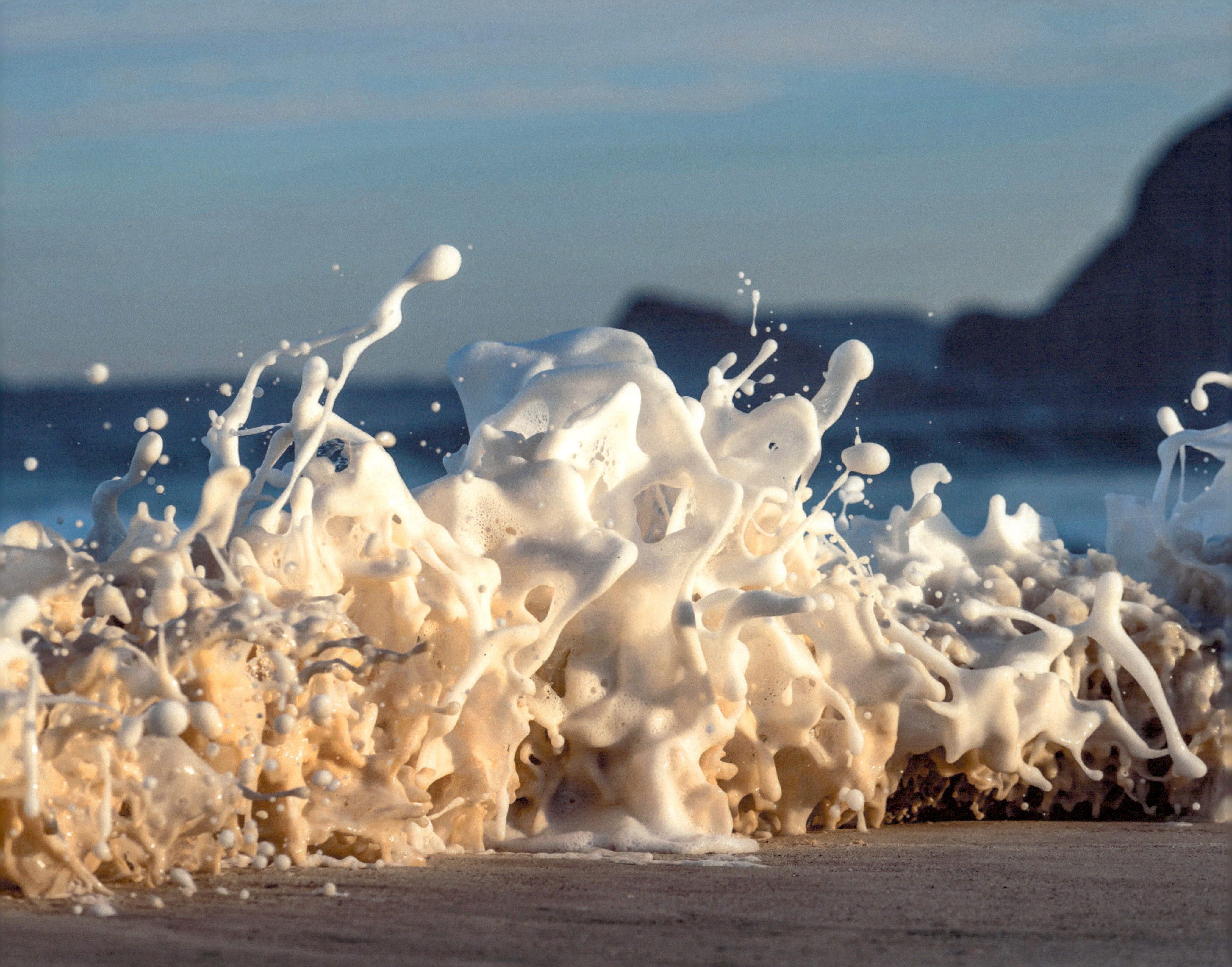

Freeze Frame

A liquid-framed view

snapped by one, shared with many

before it shatters.

Seclusion

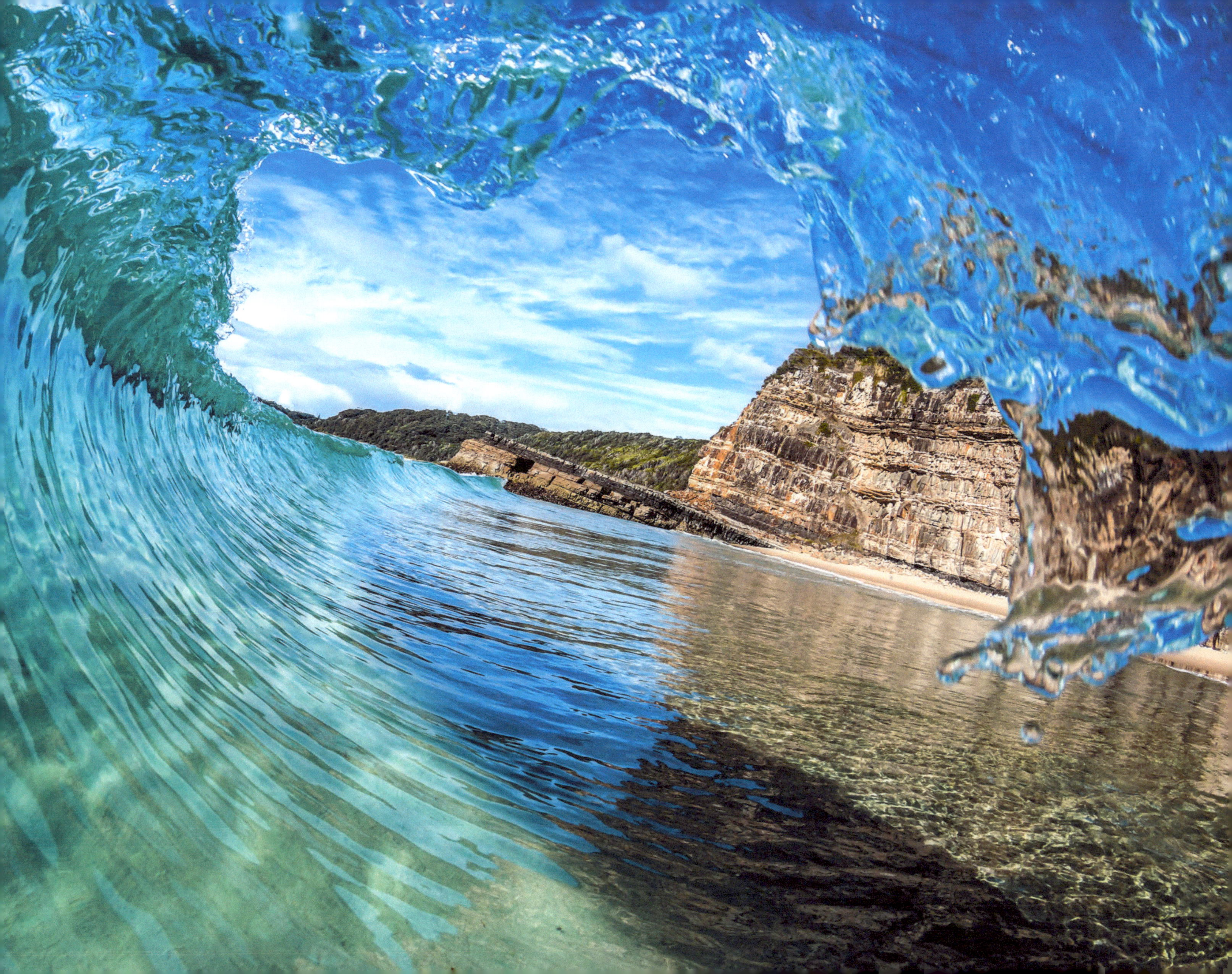

Mr. Greenback

What are the chances

you'll change the ways of your world

for a guy like me?

Greenback, Seal Rocks

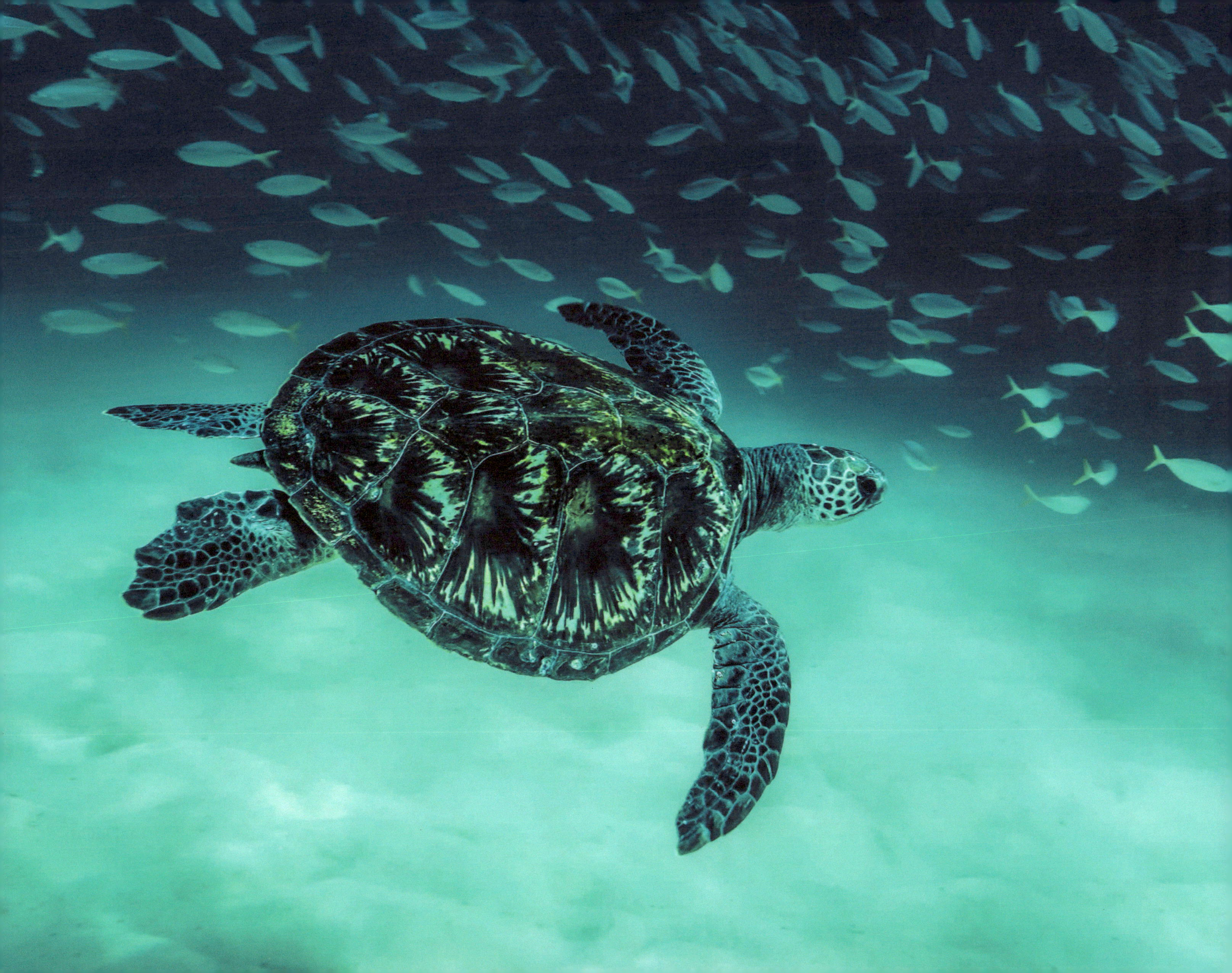

Perilous Beauty

She builds and she breaks
wielding great power beneath
perilous beauty.

Last Light

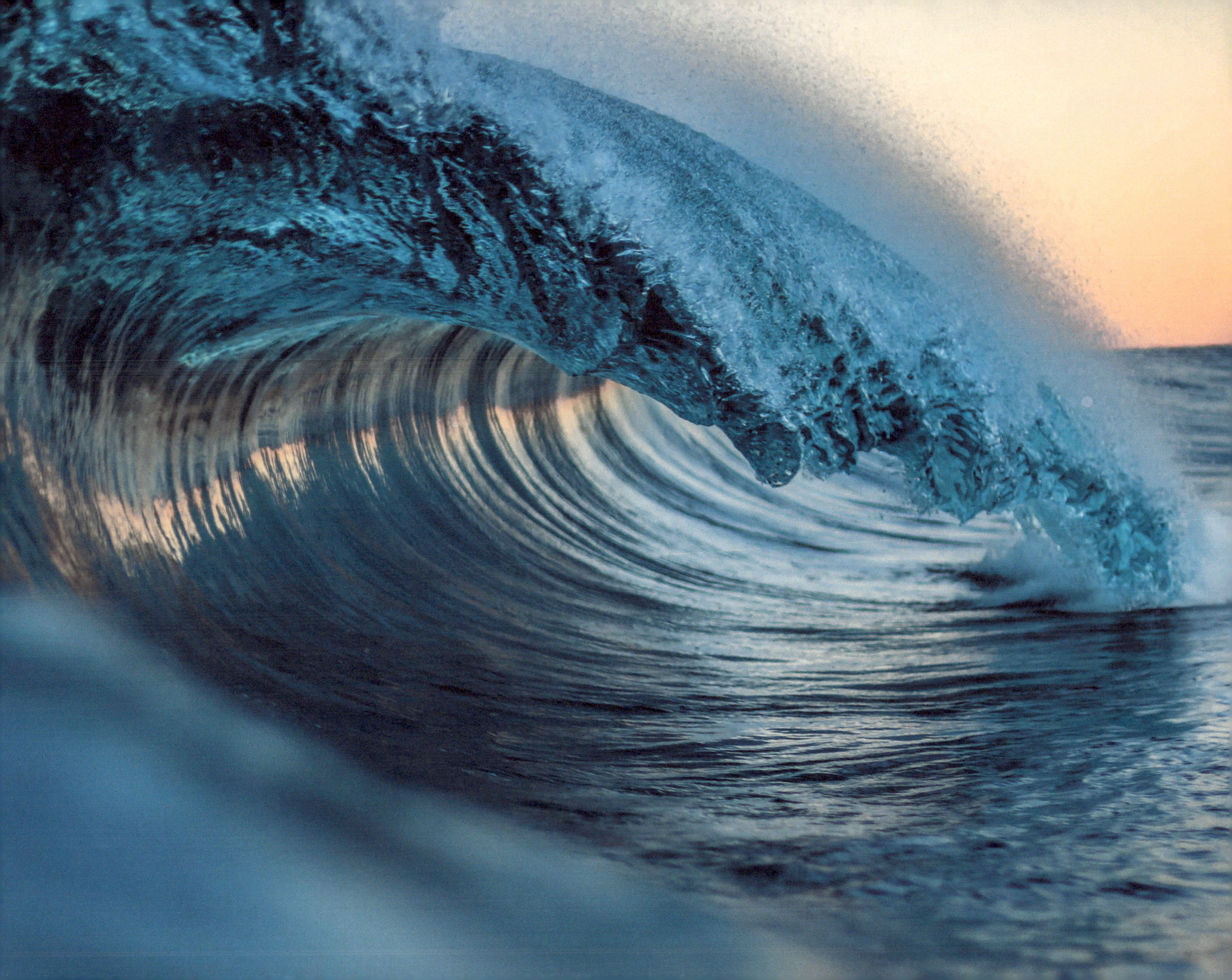

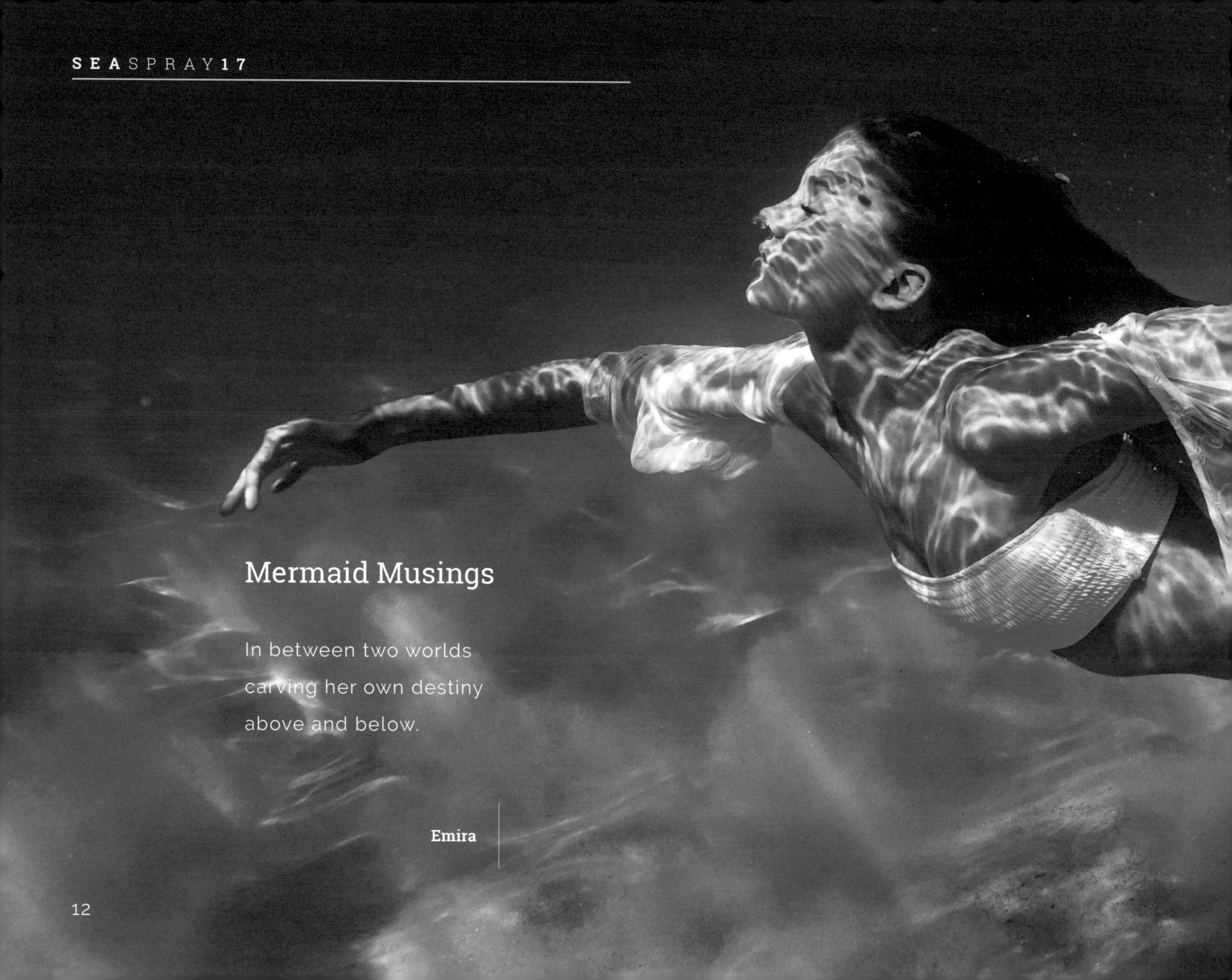

Mermaid Musings

In between two worlds
carving her own destiny
above and below.

Emira

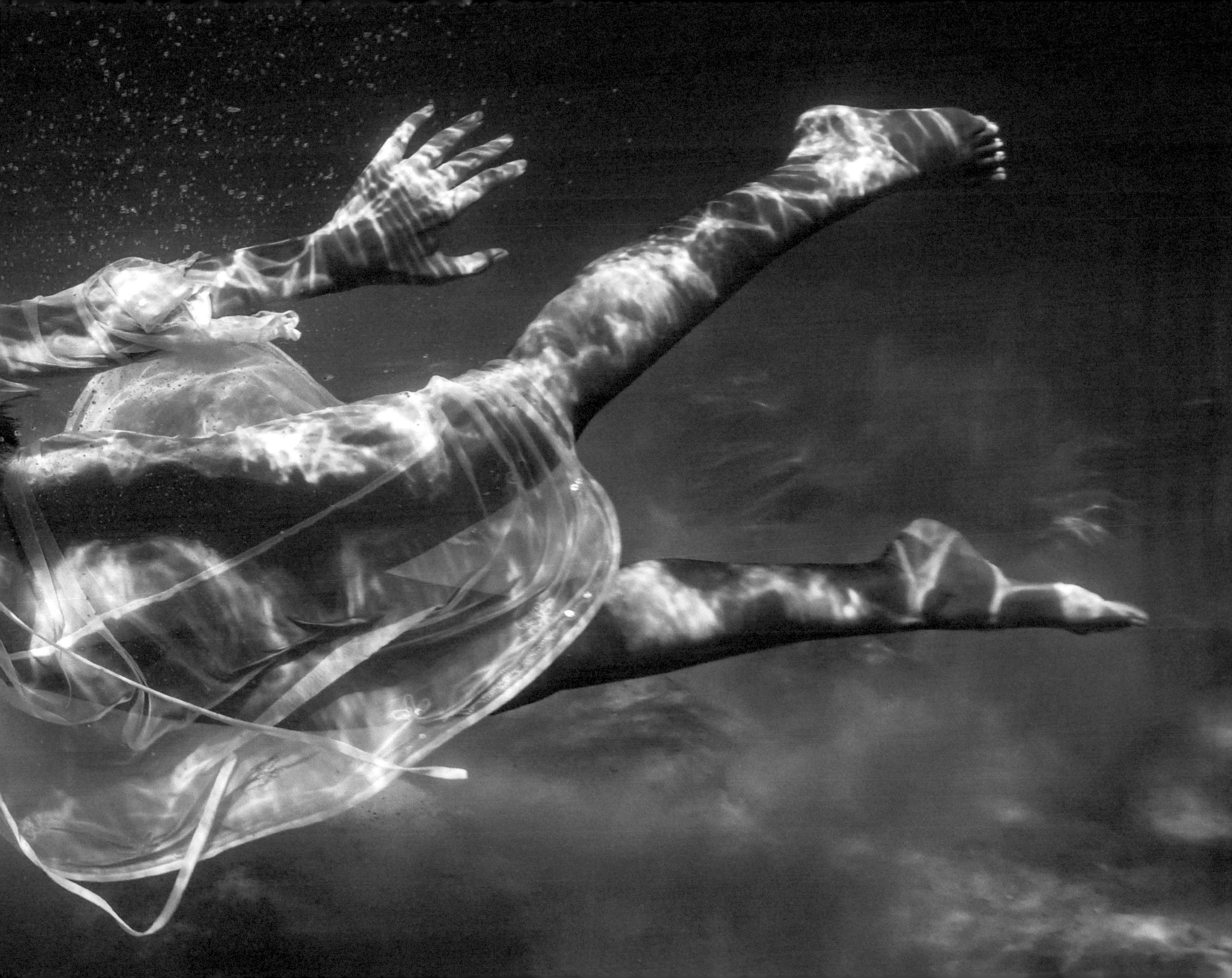

Roar

King of the Ocean
deep in waving greens he hides
protecting his pride.

Lion's Roar

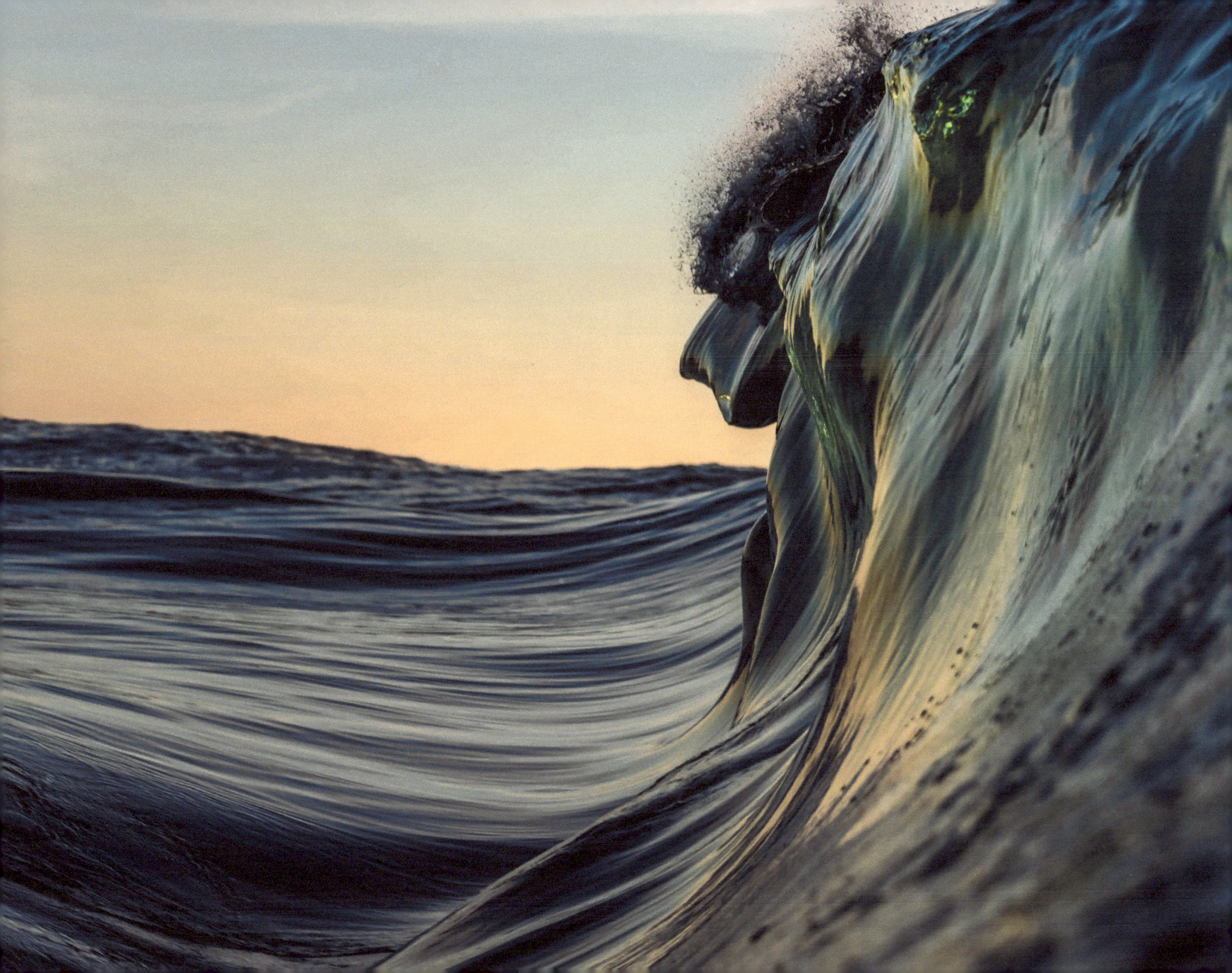

Into the Mystic

Between sky and sea
magic is no mystery
reach out and touch it.

Sunrise Tide Pool

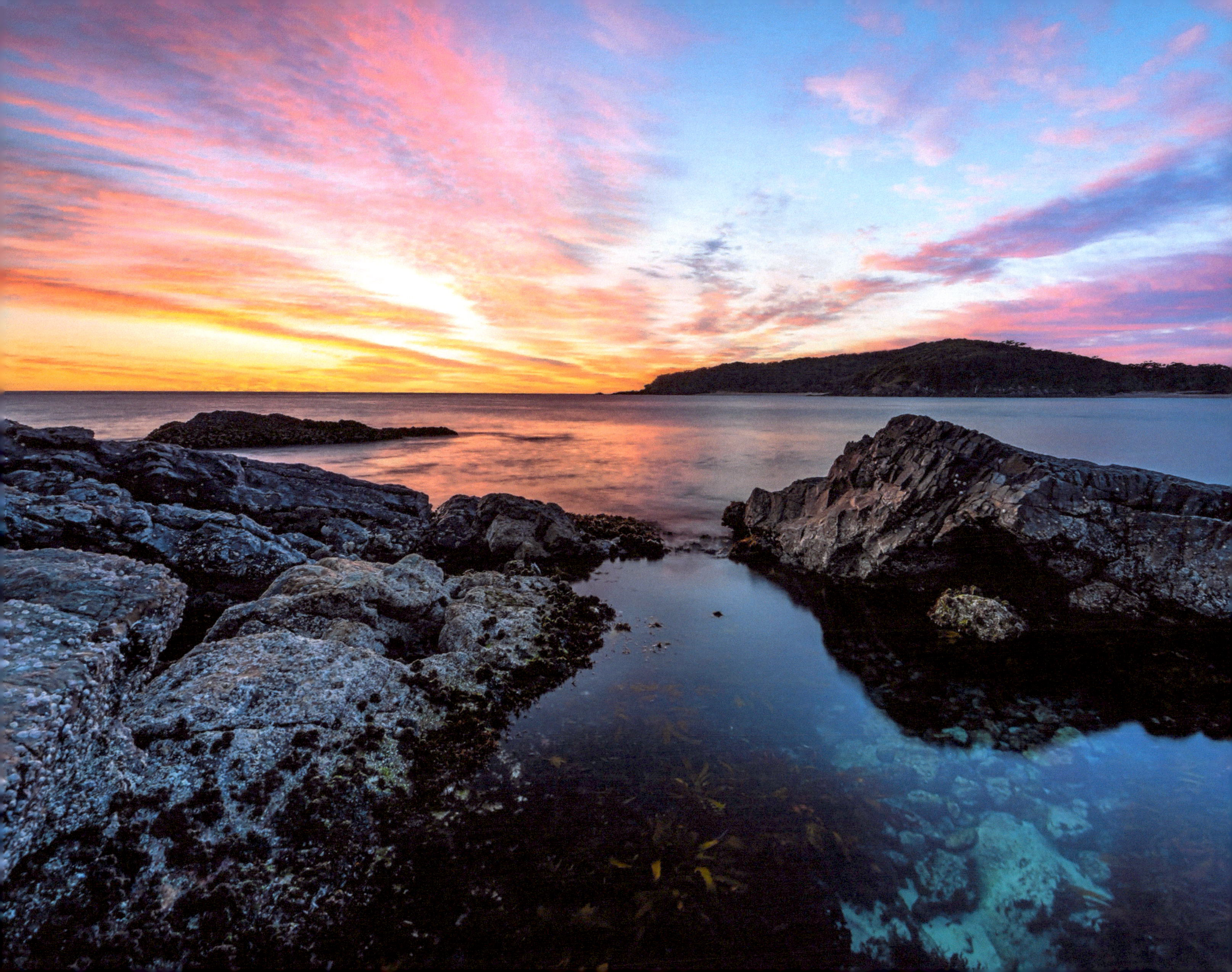

Surrounded

He found his true self

in the spotlight, surrounded

by curious crowds.

Swallows' Cave

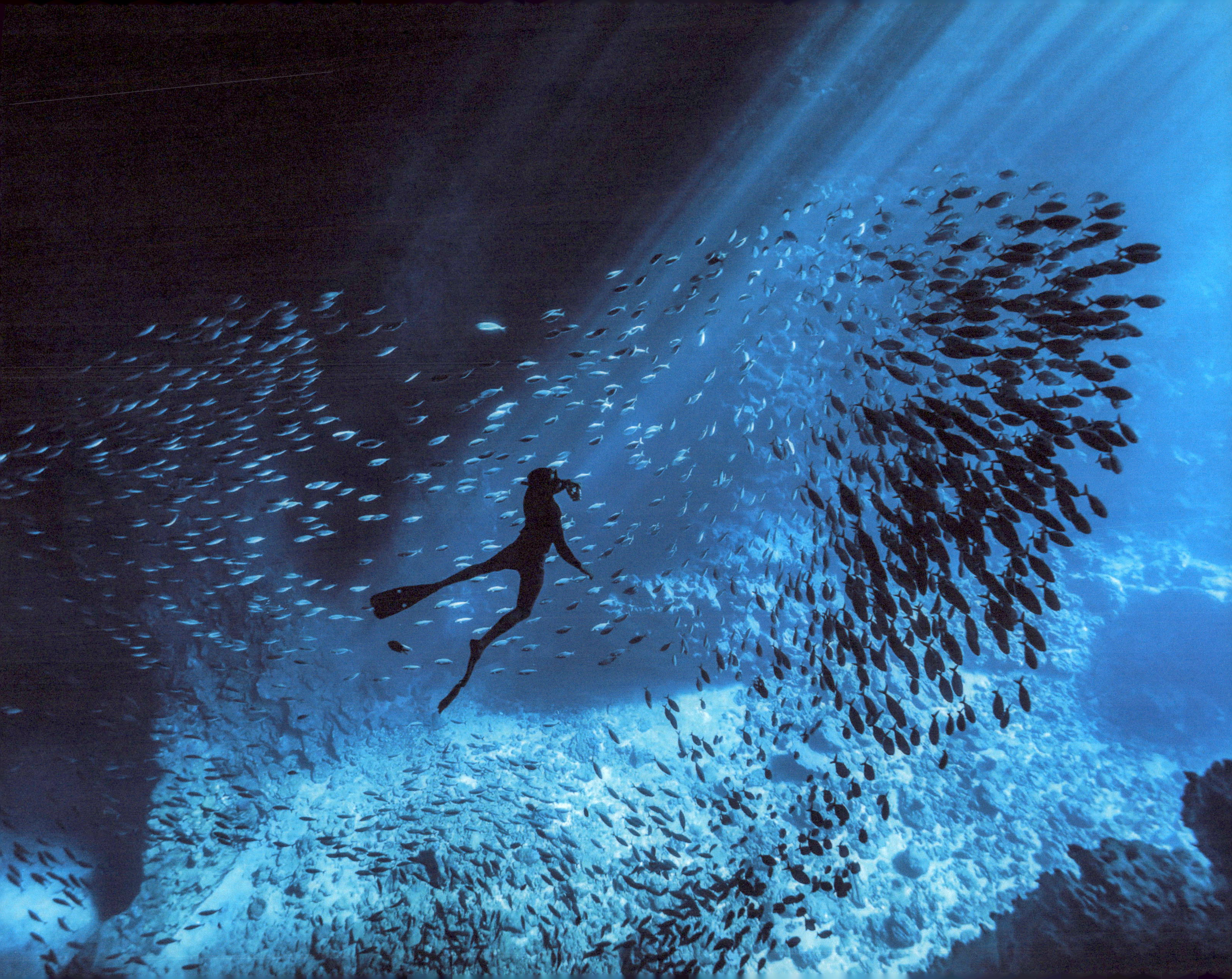

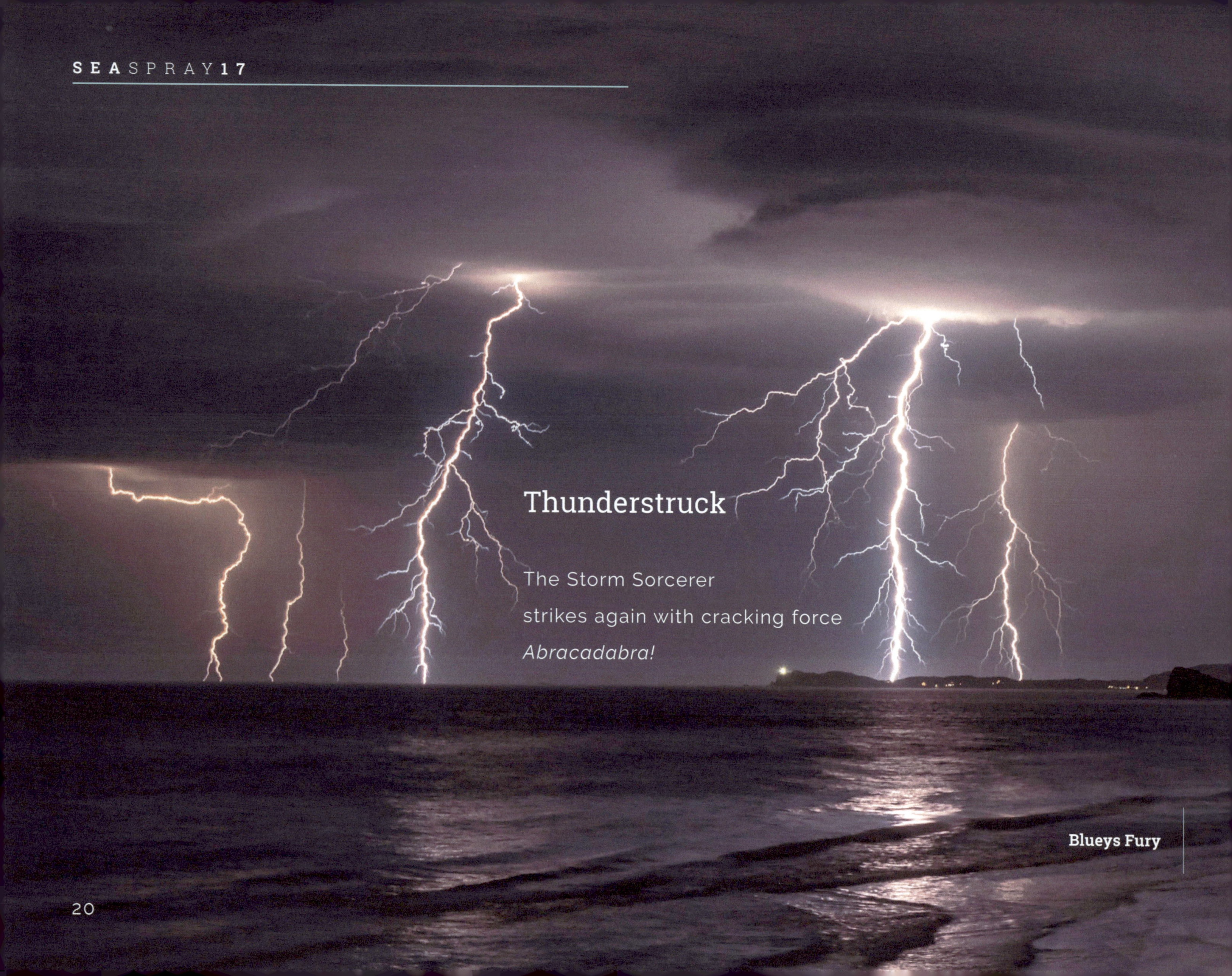

Thunderstruck

The Storm Sorcerer

strikes again with cracking force

Abracadabra!

Blueys Fury

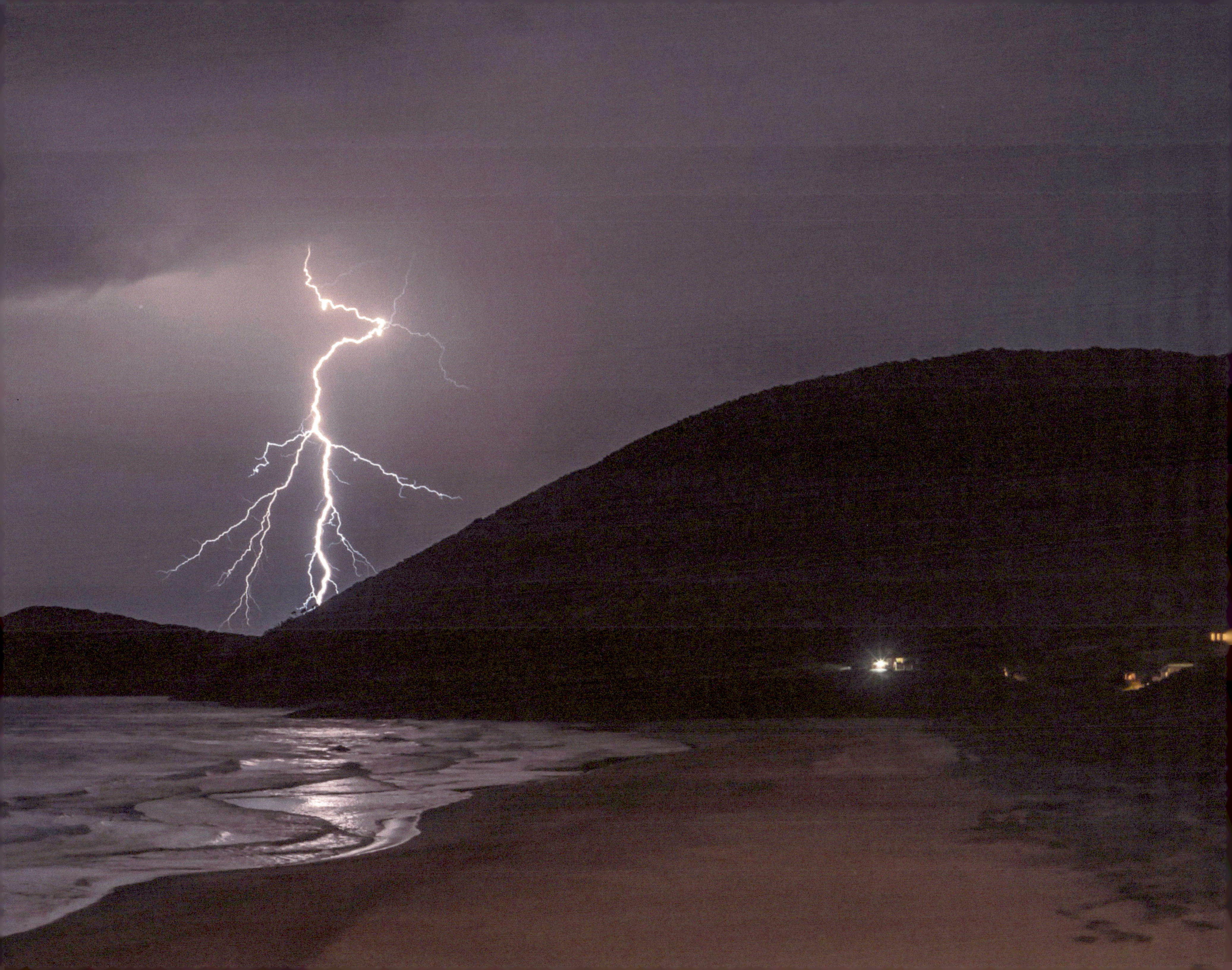

Lessons from the Sea

Constant ebb and flow.

Will she ever let me go?

Push. Pull. Give. Take. Be.

Clarity

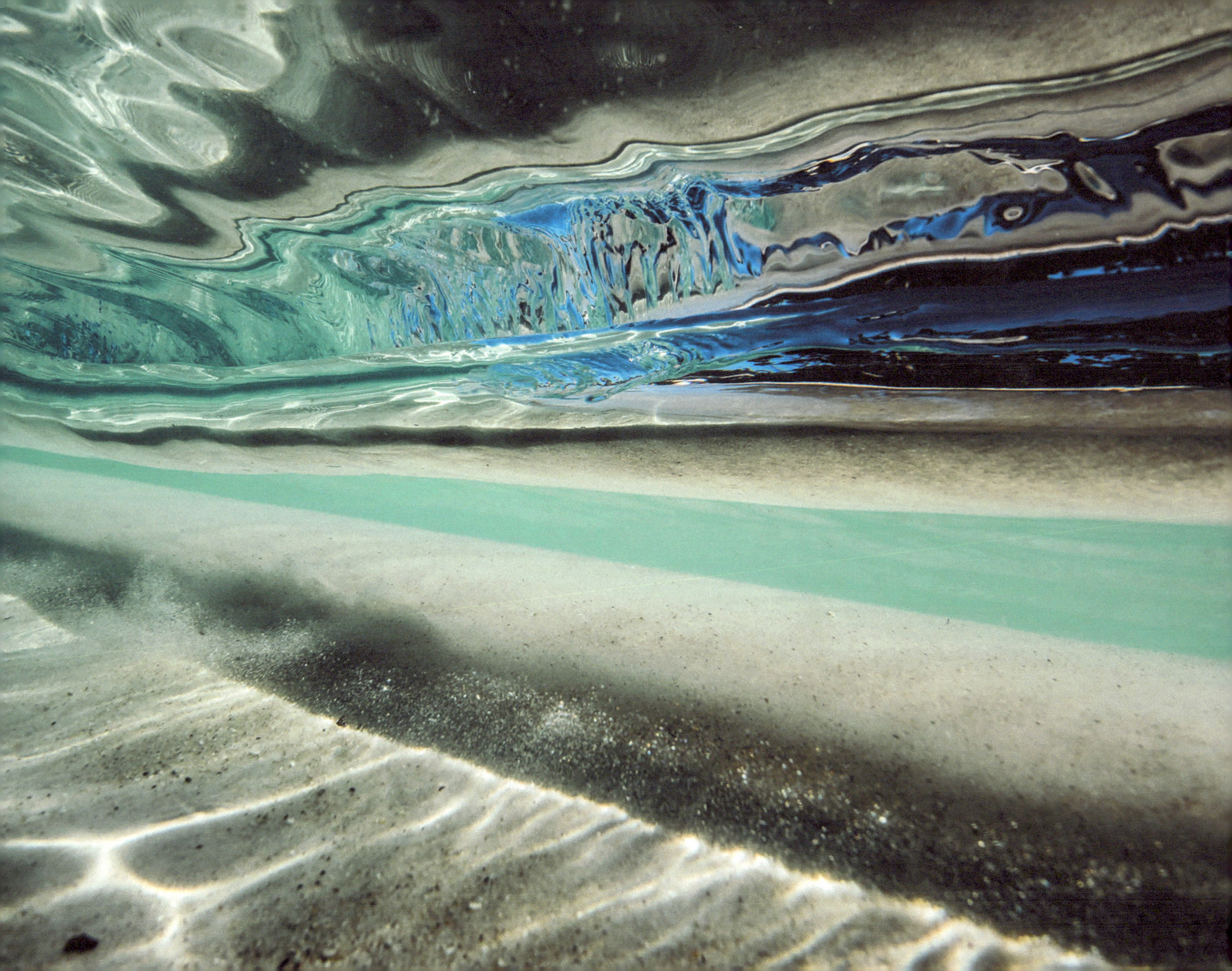

Sea Salutation

We remember them
in the gold last light of day
and in the morning.

Emerald Wall

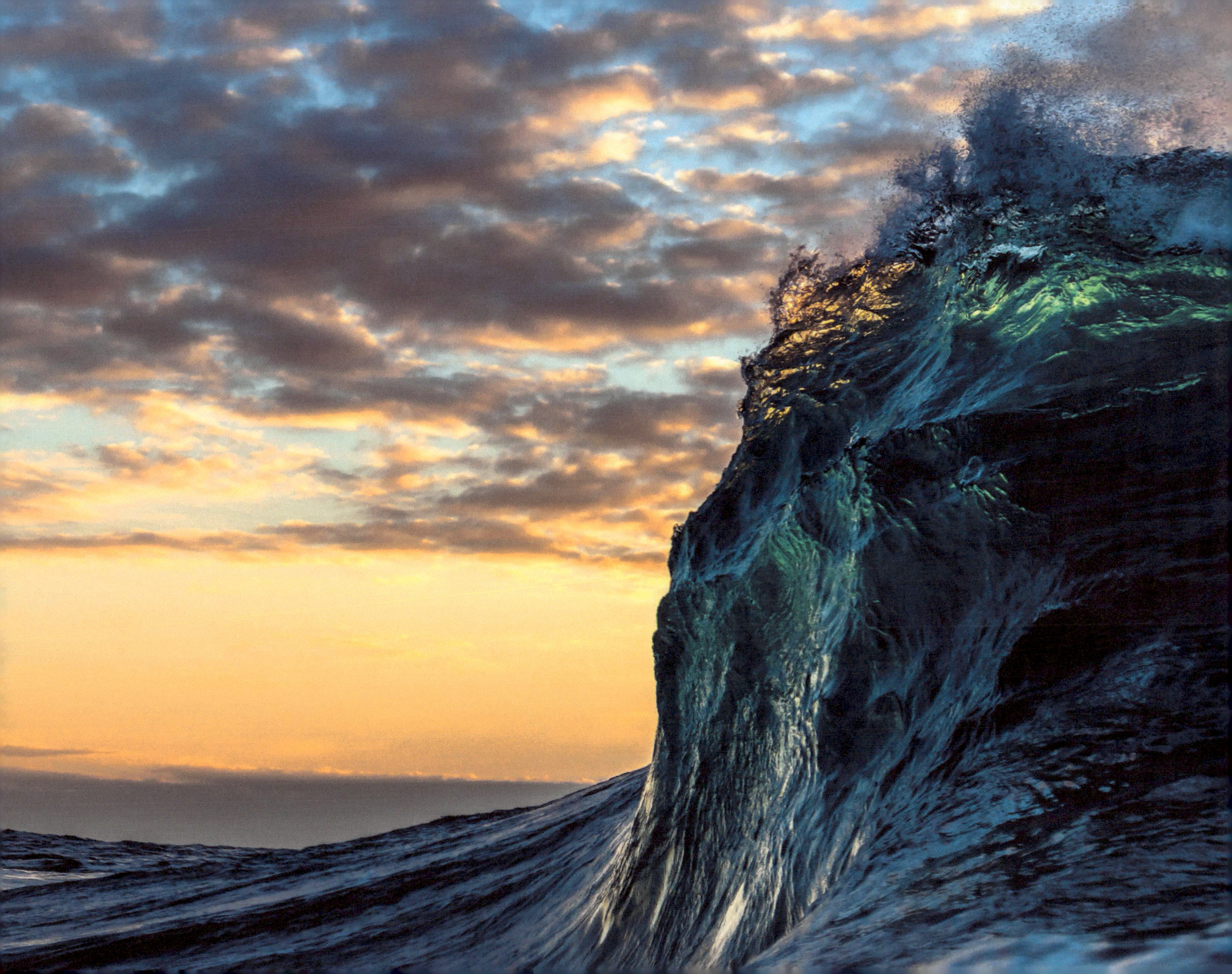

Swim

Go on, dive in, swim.
Only with salt in your eyes
will you see clearly.

Pure Bliss

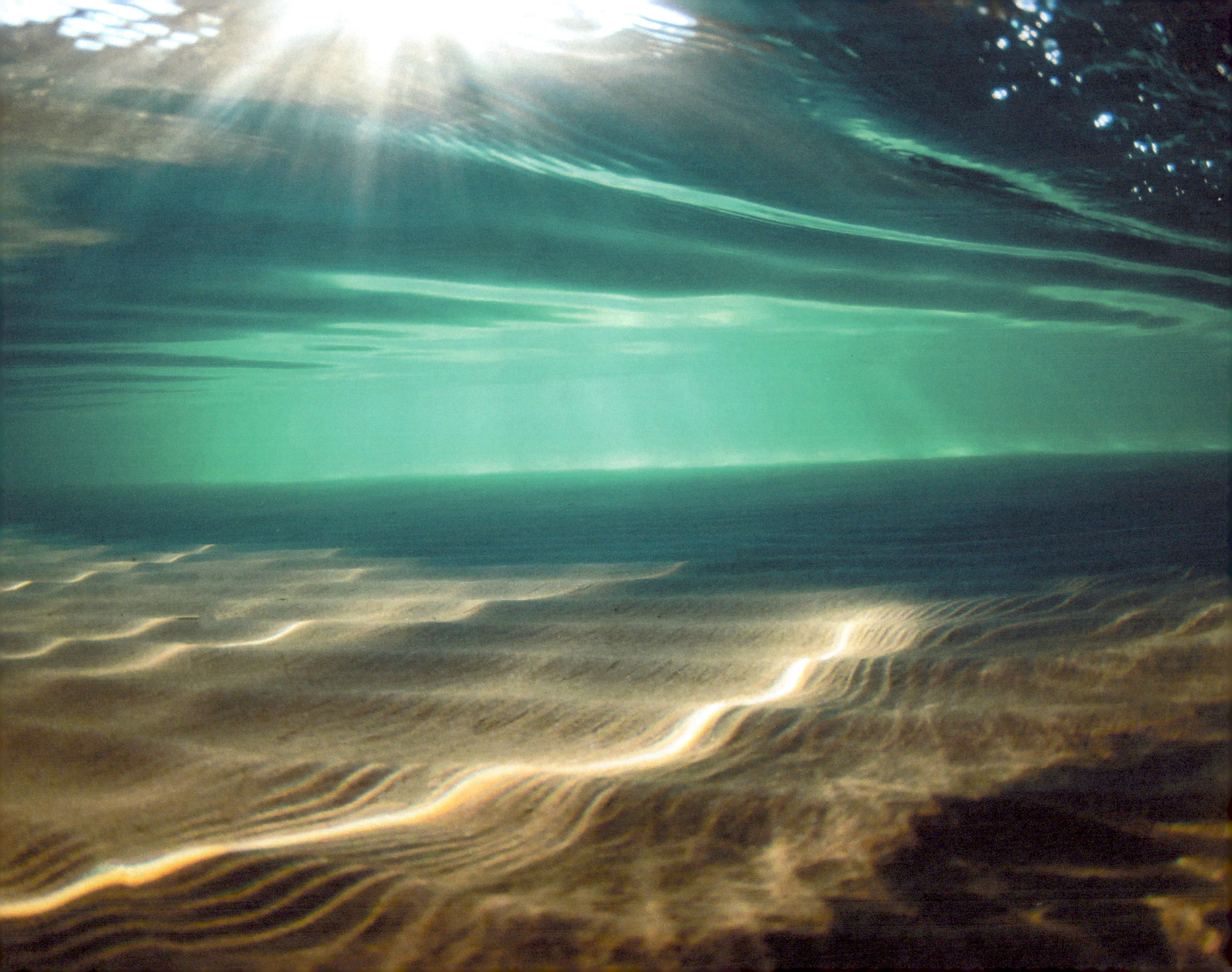

With You

When I am with you
my heart reminds me of its
vulnerable might.

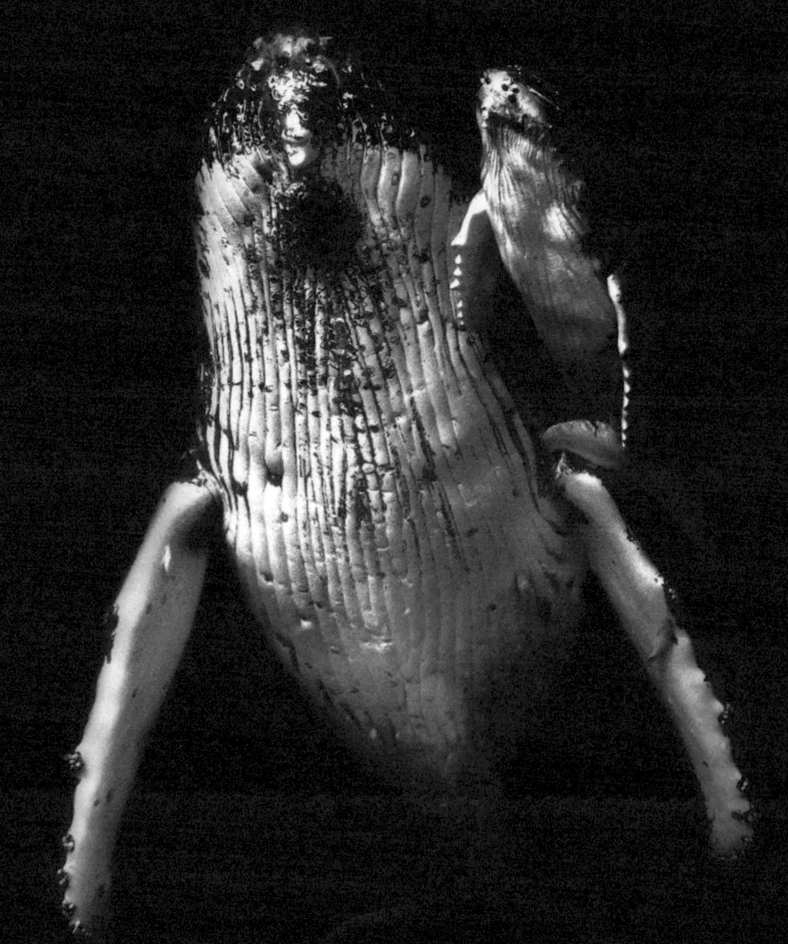

Mum & Calf

Your Lead

From the biggest breach

to the darkest dive down deep

I'll follow your lead.

Descend

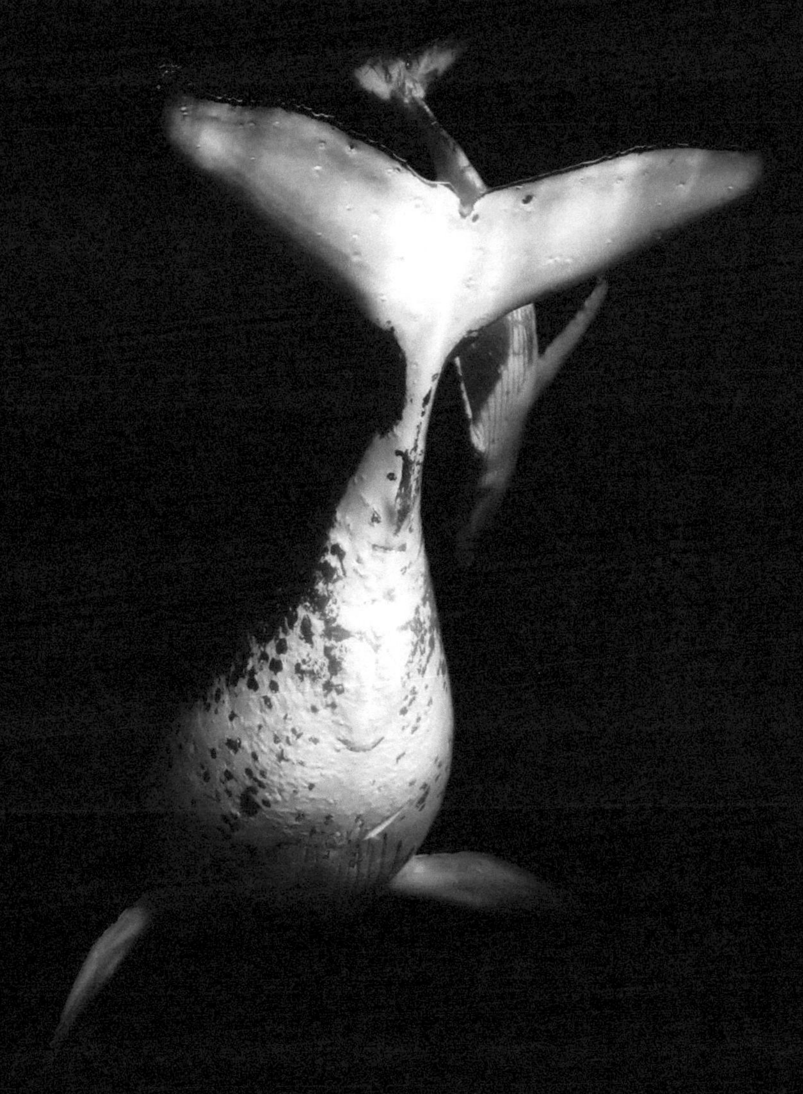

The Dive Jive

Shake, rattle and roll
jiving, alive and thriving
rock on, reef, rock on.

Pacific Rings

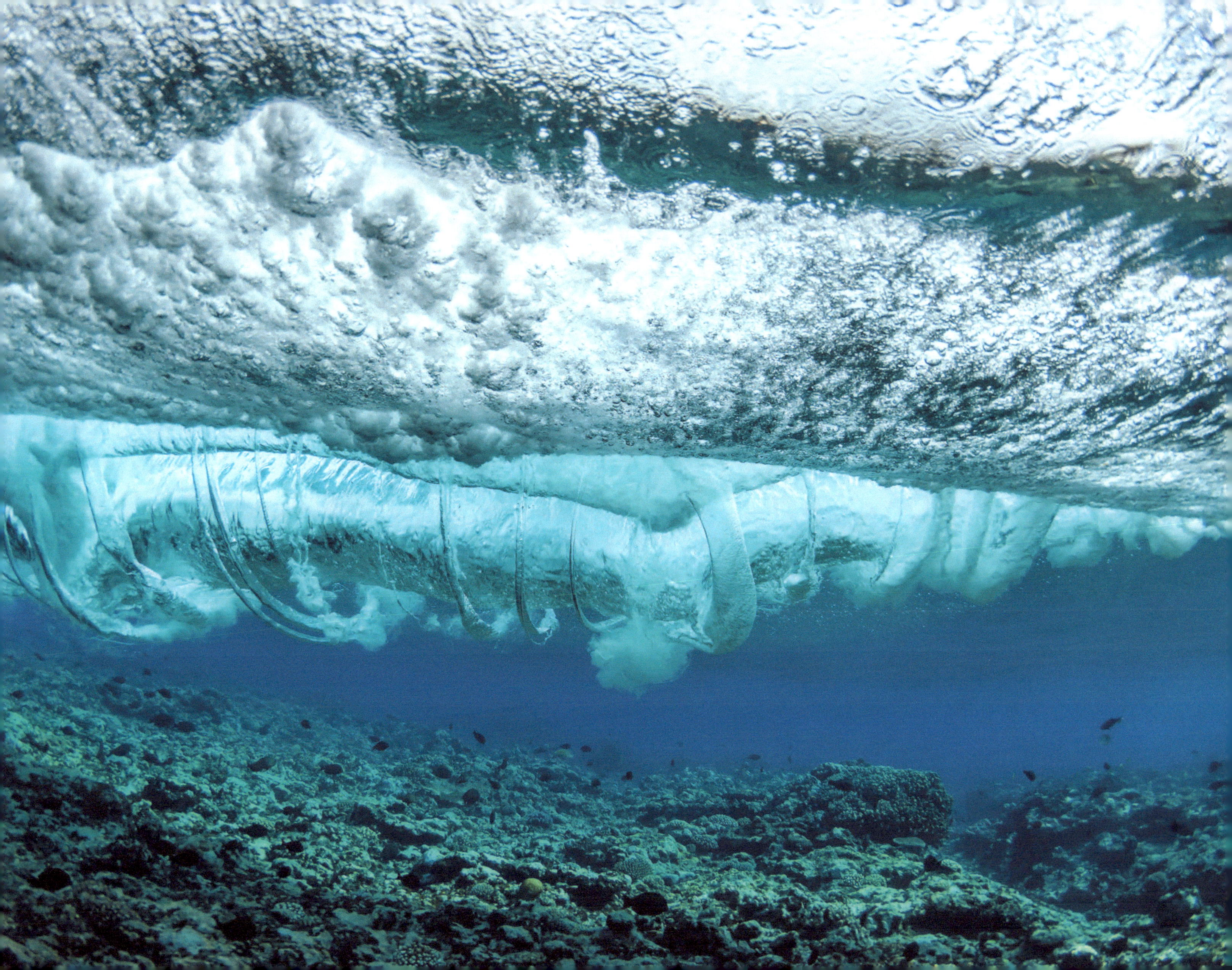

Heart of Gold

Within her wild ways
raging, raw and unashamed
shines a heart of gold.

Sunset Love

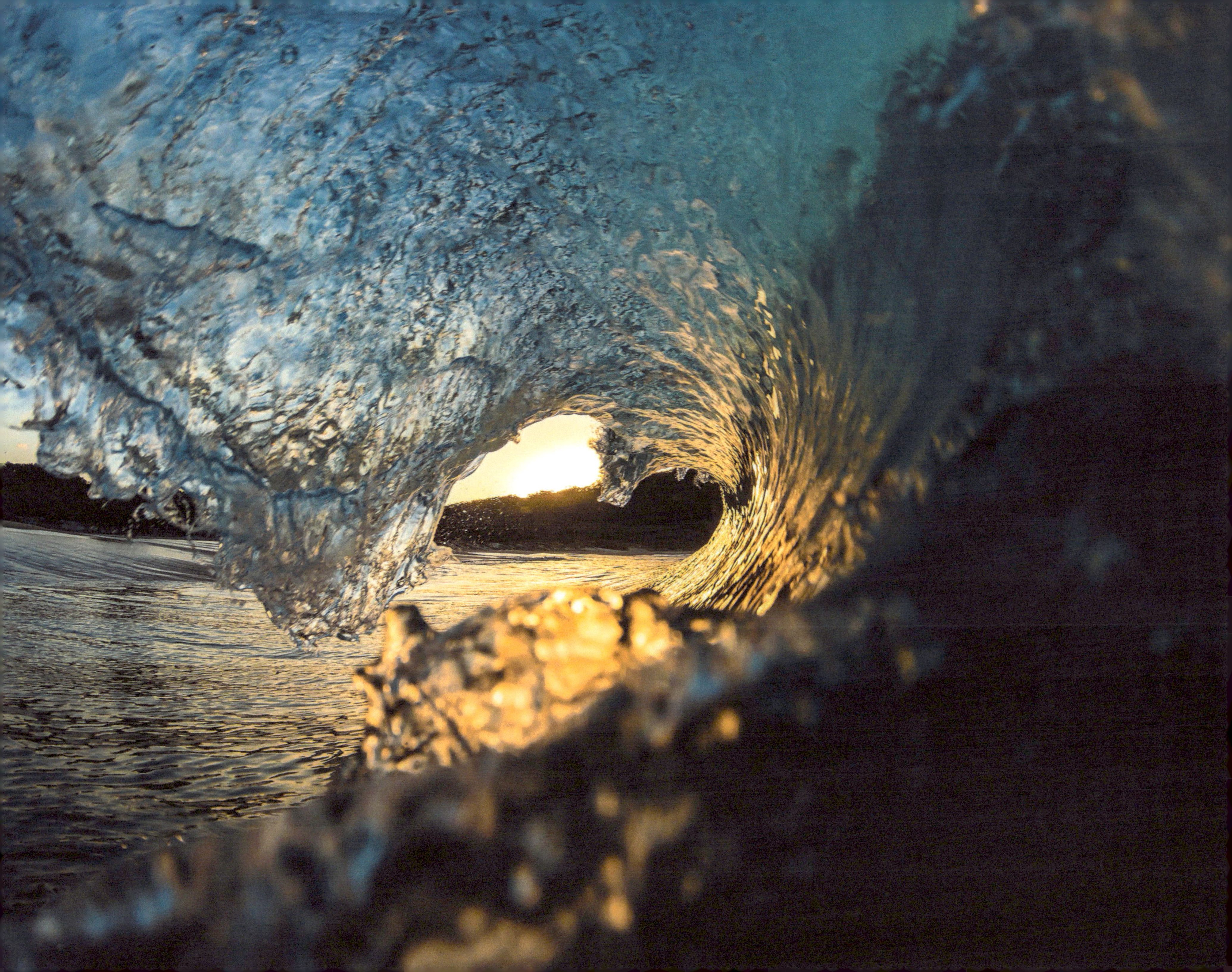

Wild and Free

Strong and wild and free

vital life rushing forward

toward extinction.

Triceratops

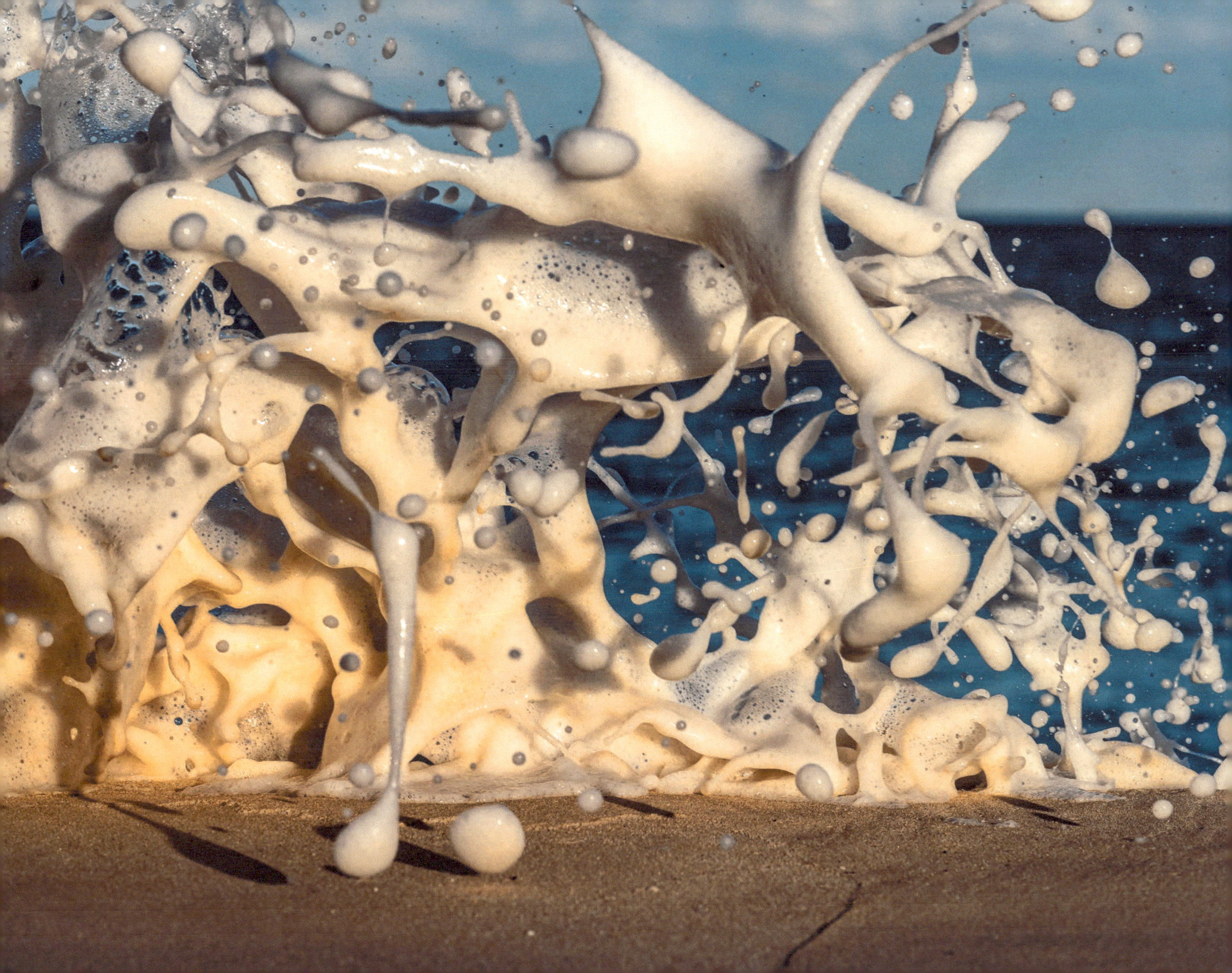

ABOUT **KIAN BATES**

Kian Bates is a multi-award-winning photographer with a passion for the ocean.

Starting with a waterproof camera in high school, Kian has developed his craft by experimenting with a series of cameras and lenses. From this passion, Raw Edge Photography was born.

Kian is constantly amazed by the view from behind the lens, both above and below the surface. No two waves ever break the same way: their unique formations and ever-changing light allow Kian to be creative with his craft. He finds sharing these captured moments in time very rewarding.

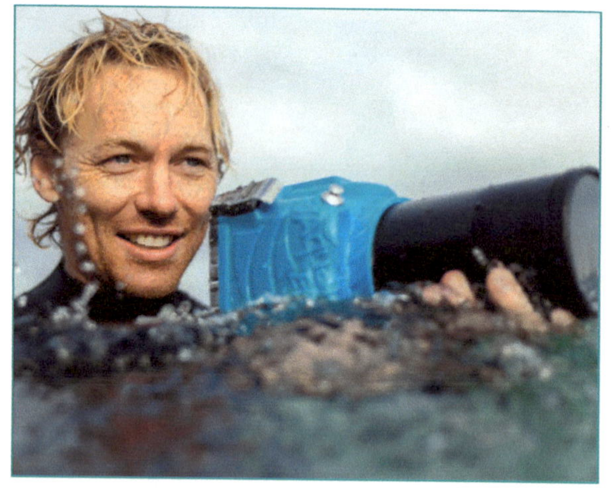

Pacific Palms in NSW is the perfect spot on the Australian coastline for Kian, his wife Ashley and their family to call home, as well as to operate their Raw Edge Gallery, where Kian's photographic art is displayed in a range of large formats. Being surrounded by such an incredible coastline means there is a never-ending source of photographic inspiration and opportunity.

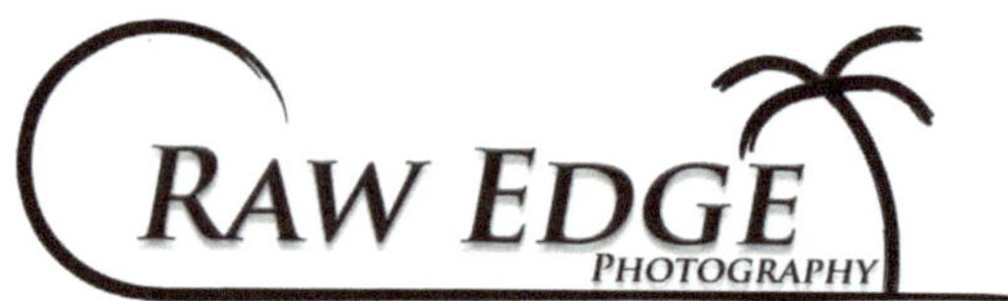

Visit www.rawedgephotography.com.au
to view Kian's latest photographs, shop his full range of photographic artworks and access free downloadable resources, including Kian's top tips on taking terrific ocean photography.

Dannika Patterson is an award-winning writer with a passion for connecting families to nature.

Through her writing Dannika seeks to educate, uplift, spark curiosity, inspire imagination and open relatable conversations. Her work has been published in Australia and internationally, across a wide range of media.

Her debut children's picture book, *Jacaranda Magic*, was released in 2018 and she was the recipient of the MBC Queenslander of the Year Award for 'Contribution to the Arts in Queensland' for 2019.

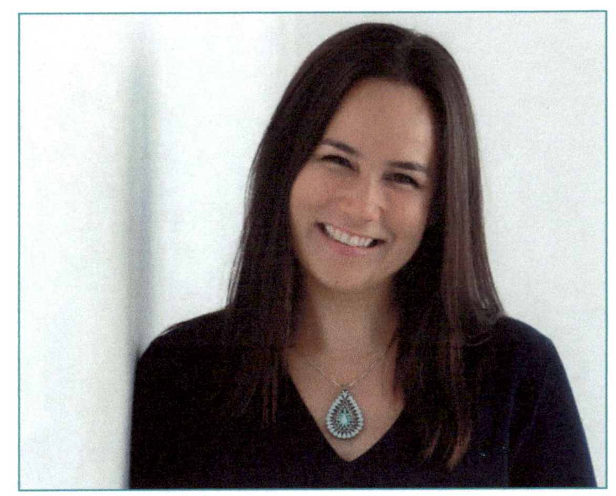

When she's not writing, Dannika loves to immerse herself in a good book or adventure outdoors with her family. She lives with her husband, two children and a hive of native Australian bees, beside the bay in Brisbane.

Visit www.dannikapatterson.com
to check out Dannika's other titles, book an author visit or writing workshop and access free downloadable resources, including Teachers' Notes and tips for writing haiku poetry.

What would happen if
your own imagination
got swept out to sea?

- KB & DP

www.ingramcontent.com/pod-product-compliance
Lightning Source LLC
Chambersburg PA
CBHW042023050726
47602CB00009B/149